C000265145

The

Kingfisher Book

of

PRESSED

FLOWERS

Kingfisher Books, Grisewood & Dempsey Ltd,
Elsley House, 24-30 Great Titchfield Street,
London W1P 7AD

This edition published in 1992 by Kingfisher Books.

This book previously was included in The Compendium of Pressed Flowers
published in 1991 by Kingfisher Books.

Copyright © Grisewood & Dempsey Ltd, 1991

All rights reserved. No part of this publication may be reproduced,
stored in a retrieval system or transmitted by any means, electronic,
mechanical, photocopying or otherwise without the prior permission
of the publisher.

ISBN 0 86272 883 5

Design · Design Eye Ltd
Editor · Gwen Edmunds
Photography · Paul Forrester
Colour illustration · Antonia Enthoven
Line illustration · West One Arts
Species illustrations by Peter Chesterton, John Davis
and Colin Emberson

Printed and bound in Hong Kong

The

Kingfisher Book

of

PRESSED

FLOWERS

JILL THOMAS

Kingfisher Books

$\mathcal{C}$ O N T E N T S

$\mathcal{I}$ NTRODUCTION

Everyone who loves flowers will appreciate this practical guide to the art and craft of flower pressing. Whether you're a complete beginner or already an enthusiast, it's designed to help you make the most of a fascinating pastime which allows you to enjoy the beauty of your favourite flowers all year round.

As all pressed flower enthusiasts quickly discover, one of the nicest things about their hobby is that they can use a huge variety of plants that are all ready to hand. You don't need to seek out rare or exotic specimens: everything you need is growing in your own or your friends' gardens, or can be found on a country walk or in the park. Even the humblest weeds can press surprisingly well, so you need never run short of material.

There's information on all aspects of flower pressing, including suitable flowers to press, picking and preparing them, using your flower press, and handling and storing your collection. This is followed by basic design guidelines and a range of attractive ideas for decorative ways to use pressed flower designs. These include everything from simple bookmarks and greetings cards to full-scale pictures, and many will make very welcome gifts for family and friends. There's also a special section on pressed flowers for children, although older children in particular will find many of the ideas in the main part of the book well within their capabilities.

Even if you think you have no artistic talent, the ideas in the following pages – plus a little inspiration from the flowers themselves – will soon have you creating your own pressed flower originals.

Bring orchis, bring the foxglove spire,
The little speedwell's darling blue,
Deep tulips dash'd with fiery dew,
Laburnum's dropping wells of fire.

Alfred, Lord Tennyson

TOOLS AND TECHNIQUES

One of the pleasures of working with pressed flowers is that much of the equipment needed can be found in most households. As you progress, you may want to spend a little more money on frames, mounts and backing materials. But to start with, once you have your flower press there will be very little additional expense especially as your main requirement, the flowers, should be free.

BASICS FOR PRESSING

If you intend to press flowers in any quantity, you will need plenty of blotting paper – white is the best colour. A pair of sharp scissors and a craft knife with a retractable blade are essential for trimming plant material before putting it in the press, for trimming items while arranging your designs and for cutting card and mounts.

Pressed flowers are delicate objects and a pair of blunt-nosed tweezers is useful for picking them up and moving them about. Very tiny and fragile blooms can be picked up with the moistened tip of a paintbrush. This, or a cocktail stick, is also helpful when arranging flowers on their backing material.

Finally, try to equip yourself with several old telephone directories. These are quite invaluable, both as D.I.Y. flower presses and for storing pressed flowers and leaves.

BASICS FOR MAKING UP DESIGNS

To make up a design the first thing needed is a smooth
dust-free surface which can be wiped clean. A large sheet
of plastic such as a pastry board is ideal – otherwise use a
smooth wooden board or a sheet of oilcloth.

To make up the design you will need a backing material:
paper, card or fabric – whichever is most appropriate
to the work; coloured pens and pencils for sketching out
the design, drawing borders etc. and a ruler.

All designs will require gluing; the best type of glue is a
latex adhesive. This can be applied in tiny blobs to the
back of the flowers and leaves using a cocktail stick or, for
larger areas, a small paintbrush or cotton bud. Cotton
buds are also good for nudging flowers into position and
for mopping up any spilt or smeared glue. You will also
need an adhesive suitable for gluing paper and card – the
solid stick type is the easiest to use.

All flower designs, even the simplest greeting card, are
much better protected by some form of sealing agent. The
easiest and cheapest to obtain is the sticky-backed library
film used for covering books, though it does require some
practice to apply neatly. Alternatives are acetate film,
which must be glued separately, varnish, or, for pressed
flower pictures, glass. All these items, together with
backing materials, mounts and frames, will be described
in more detail later in the book.

Blotting paper	Ruler
Sharp scissors	Card (plain and coloured)
Craft knife	Paper (plain and coloured)
Blunt-nose tweezers	Cotton buds
Paintbrush	Cocktail sticks
Telephone directories	Clear acetate film
Glue (Copydex or similar)	Clear library film (matt or gloss)
Glue (solid stick)	Varnish
Coloured pencils/pens	Large wipeable board

PICKING FLOWERS FOR PRESSING

Pick only perfect plant specimens for pressing; any
bruising or flaws in the petals will show up badly once the
flowers are pressed. It is best to pick on a dry, sunny day –
choose a time when the dew has dried, but before fragile
petals begin to flag in the sunshine. Pick a good selection
of fully-open flowers, half-open flowers and buds for
contrast of shape, also plenty of leaves and stems.

Most picking and pressing is done in the spring and
summer months when conditions are at their best and the
widest range of plant material is available. But there are
interesting and suitable flowers and leaves available all
year round and these can be picked and pressed quite
successfully provided this one rule is followed: *never* put
any damp material in the flower press, or you will end up
with stained, mouldy specimens.

Material should be put in the press as soon as possible
after picking. Once flowers have begun to flag they will
never regain their crisp, clear outlines. Flowers picked
away from home can be kept fresh and undamaged in a
plastic snap-top bag or a polythene box with an airtight
seal. A travelling press is a useful piece of equipment if you
are going to be away from home for some time (p.12).

Preparing Flowers for Pressing

Picked flowers should first be sorted through to make
sure no grubs or insects lurk in their petals. For pressing,
lay the flowers on sheets of absorbent paper; blotting
paper is best, but paper kitchen towels can be used – try
to avoid the type with very marked corrugations or the
flowers will end up with bumpy petals. Very small,
delicate flowers can even be pressed between a double
thickness of good-quality lavatory paper.

The best way to press most flowers is face downwards
on the paper, unless they are to be pressed in profile
(p.11). Remember, the flatter the flower, the better the
final result will be, so it's a good idea to remove all
unnecessary parts like projecting calyxes and seedboxes
which could spoil the final shape.

If flowers are being pressed full face, stems should be
removed as these can show through the semi-transparent
dried petals and do not look very attractive. Stems and
foliage should be pressed separately as they are usually
bulkier than flowers. Specimens inside the press should
not touch or overlap.

Trumpet flowers *should be sliced in half and pressed in profile; small blooms can be pressed full face.*

Leaves and Stems *should be pressed separately from flowers as they tend to be bulkier and may need greater pressure.*

Multi-petalled flowers *normally need to be taken apart for pressing and then reassembled in designs. Rosebuds can be sliced in half and pressed in profile. Single species roses such as the shrub rose* rosa rubrifolia *can be pressed whole.*

Spray flowers *can be pressed on their stems making an attractive shape. Individual flowers can also be pressed.*

Multi-florets *can be pressed whole if they are small or can be divided into individual florets; they are very useful in the making up of designs.*

Simple flowers *are usually pressed full face but calyxes, seedboxes and stems should all be removed.*

Trimming and preparing material. Use a very sharp knife to cut flowers and other plant material. Material of different thicknesses, whole flowers, petals, stems and leaves should be pressed separately to ensure an even pressing.

Trumpet flowers, flowers with an interesting shape in profile and many sorts of buds are best pressed in profile. Slice in half lengthwise with a sharp knife. Both halves of the flower can be used.

Multi-petalled flowers need to be systematically taken apart. The petals can be used to rebuild the original shape of the flower or can be used individually as part of any design.

Pressing Times

The longer a flower is pressed, the better it will keep its colour. In an ideal world flowers picked in the spring and summer would not be looked at until the winter months. It's unlikely that this will happen, but for best results, flowers should be left undisturbed in their presses for at least six to eight weeks.

If the press is stored in a warm place, such as the top of a central heating boiler or an airing cupboard, pressing time can be reduced to 2-3 weeks but the flowers must have been perfectly dry when they were put in the press.

The way to tell if a flower is properly dried and ready to use is to pick it up by its stem, if it has one, or by the tip of a petal. If it stands up stiffly it is ready; if it flops it needs longer in the press.

Pressing in a Hurry

Cool Iron The pressing process can be speeded up using a cool iron. Place your flowers or leaves between a few sheets of blotting paper and press them gently with a low iron. The specimens can then be transferred to a press for a few days to dry out completely.

This is a good method for dealing with damp material, to prevent it going mouldy in the press.

Microwave The microwave can be useful to speed up the pressing of more robust material; autumn leaves and herbs such as rosemary give good results.

Prepare the flowers or foliage for pressing as normal and place them between two sheets of blotting paper which have been cut to fit the microwave turntable. Put the blotting paper 'sandwich' on the turntable and weight it down with a plate.

Half a minute on low seems to be sufficient to drive the moisture out of most specimens; any longer or higher seems to 'cook' them, turning them brown and shrivelled. There is a serious risk of the blotting paper catching fire so watch what is happening all the time and switch the oven off at the first sign of charring.

The paper and flowers should then be put in a press. The flowers should be ready for use in about a week.

Labelling

It's a very good idea to label all specimens as they are put into the press. As each layer of flowers and leaves is prepared for pressing, *write down* what they are on a slip of paper, date it and tuck it into the press with them so that it can be read at a glance when you look at the press.

Points to remember before you press

1 Use dry, perfect flowers and foliage.
2 Pick over for grubs and insects.
3 Lay flowers on blotting paper. Do not let them touch.
4 Place flowers of the same thickness on one sheet of paper.
5 Place flowers face down or in profile.
6 Remove hard seedcases, calyxes and stems.
7 Put leaves and stems on a separate sheet.

USING YOUR FLOWER PRESS

The basic technique of flower pressing is very simple. The flowers are placed between layers of absorbent paper, separated by card or other material such as newspaper, and then weighted so that the moisture is gradually squeezed out of them.

It is quite easy to make your own flower press – a large book and a couple of bricks will do the job. However, a custom-made press will give the best results. This is because the screws allow a uniform pressure to be applied and, as the flowers dry, the press can be gradually tightened to give a really tight squeeze.

More Ways to Press Flowers

Once you start to become seriously interested in flower pressing, and realise what a wealth of material is available, one press will certainly not be enough. The following alternatives make good temporary presses.

A heavy book

Equipment: A large, heavy book (telephone directories are ideal); newspaper; blotting paper; one or two house bricks.

This is the simplest and cheapest method of pressing flowers and several heavy books can be piled one on top of the other.

1 Trim the blotting paper and a double sheet of newspaper to twice the size of the book; fold them both in half.
2 Open out and place the blotting paper on top of the newspaper. Lay the flowers on one half of the blotting paper and fold the other half of the paper on top.
3 Slide this flower and paper sandwich between the pages of the book; repeat with as many layers as the book will hold.
4 Weight the book down with house bricks.

Pressing between boards

Equipment: 2 wooden boards of the same size (for example, sawn-off planks or old wooden chopping boards); bricks; sheets of corrugated cardboard cut to the size of the boards; blotting paper; newspapers.

This is a good way of pressing a large quantity of flowers if you have the room to spare.

1 On one board build up layers of sandwiches of corrugated card, newspaper (about 4 sheets thick) and blotting paper containing the flowers.
2 Place the second board on top and weight it down with two or more bricks, depending on the length of the board.

Travelling press

Equipment: 2 small pieces of plywood; sheets of corrugated paper; blotting paper; 2 strong elastic bands.

This press is very useful if you are collecting flowers away from home.

1 Load up the press in the normal way.
2 Hold the press firmly together using strong tight-fitting elastic bands.

Storage while Pressing

A flower press should always be stored in a dry, well-ventilated place, to prevent mildew appearing. An airing cupboard is the ideal spot but any dry, undisturbed part of the house will do – perhaps a spare bedroom. If possible keep flower presses off the floor where dust and fluff may mark their contents.

A flower press is made up of layers of blotting paper and corrugated card, held together in a wooden frame. The pressure of the press is adjustable by tightening the wing nuts.

HANDLING AND STORAGE

Handling Pressed Flowers

Pressed material should be handled as little as possible as it is brittle and easily shattered. Larger items can safely be picked up in the fingers, but use tweezers for more delicate blooms – they are far less likely to get damaged.

If flowers tend to stick to their blotting paper use the tip of a paintbrush or a cocktail stick to gently prise them from their backing.

Storing Pressed Flowers

Pressed flowers need to be stored flat, dry and out of the light. The easiest place to store them is between the pages of old telephone directories. These can then be piled up somewhere where they can remain undisturbed.

Flowers and leaves should be sorted out according to certain categories before they are stored. It is up to you to decide which would be the most useful way to store your material – by colour, size, species or whatever. However you decide to store material make sure each page is clearly labelled with its contents.

A method of storage that costs a little money, but is very convenient, is to put your flowers in envelopes or, better still, transparent paper-backed cellophane bags, inside a concertina-style file made out of stiff cardboard. Both the file compartments and the envelopes or bags themselves can be labelled with their contents. Needless to say, the file should be stored flat, not upright.

Storing material according to colour will be helpful in the making up of designs.

FLOWERS AND PLANTS FOR PRESSING

*T*here is no doubt that some flowers do press very much better than others, and those recommended in this chapter are tried and tested. If they are used as a starting point, you will soon build up a good and varied collection. Of course, once you are confident in pressing techniques you will certainly want to experiment.

Remember that the aim of the pressing process is to dry out the flower, and that the quicker it dries, the better it will retain its shape and colour. This means that, on the whole, the flatter and less succulent the flower is, the better it will press. Thick, fleshy blooms like orchids and African violets are the least likely to give good results.

Leaves, stems and grasses are equally important in the making up of designs; some of the best are listed, but again there's plenty of room for experiment. Autumn leaves keep their colours exceptionally well when pressed, being partially dried when they are collected.

Cultivated Flowers

A large number of these flowers should be available in your own or a friend's garden. However, if you do not have a garden, or are looking for flowers to press in the winter months, a good florist should be able to supply quite a number of the flowers listed.

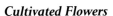

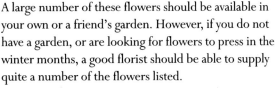

Achillea (Yarrow) The small white flowers of *A. ptarmica* 'The Pearl' are a useful size and keep their colour well.

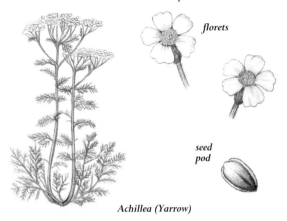

florets

seed pod

Achillea (Yarrow)

Alchemilla mollis (Lady's mantle) The tiny, acid-green flowers make attractive sprays.

Alyssum Delicate flowers to press as sprays.

Anemone blanda Blue, pink or white daisy-like flowers which can be pressed whole.

Anthemis White or pale yellow daisies which keep their colour well. Flatten or remove the domed centres before pressing. The leaves are also useful.

Cheiranthus (Wallflower) An attractive range of shades from pale yellow to deep maroon. Press individual florets.

Clematis Of the vast clematis family, the small-flowered species such as *C. montana* generally press best. Large-flowered varieties such as 'Nelly Moser' have interesting shaped petals to press individually but cannot be relied on to keep their colour.

Coreopsis The yellow and maroon daisy-like petals keep their colour well.

Cosmos An attractive range of colours. The pinks and reds are especially useful.

Crocosmia masonorum (Montbretia) The rich orange-red flowers keep their colour well. Press as sprays or individual open flowers.

Delphinium Amongst the best of blue flowers for pressing, and the pink shades are equally good.

Delphinium consolida (Larkspur) Like its relative the delphinium, all colours can be pressed successfully.

Dicentra spectabilis (Bleeding heart) Unusual pink and white flowers to press in sprays. There is also a pure white variety.

Erica (Heather) All colours press well. The hard stalks can be removed.

Eschscholzia Press these annual poppy-like flowers both whole and individual petals.

Forsythia Early yellow flowers from this common shrub.

Freesia All colours press well, as single flowers or in sprays.

Fritillaria meleagris (Snake's head fritillary) A rare wild bulb, but quite easy to grow in the garden and very beautiful. The chequered pattern on the petals shows up well after pressing.

Fritillaria meleagris (Snake's head fritillary)

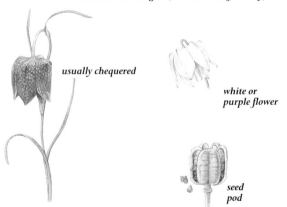

usually chequered

white or purple flower

seed pod

Fuchsia The common hardy fuchsia, *F. magellanica*, keeps its colour extremely well and is a pretty shape. The larger varieties are less good, but worth experimenting with. Most need to be taken apart before pressing.

Geranium (Crane's bill) This is the border perennial, not the bedding geranium or pelargonium. Of the many varieties, *G. endressii* 'A. T. Johnson' presses a lovely soft pink and *G. renardii* has attractive white flowers with maroon veins.

Geum chiloense The red and orange flowers fade a little when pressed, but are still very attractive and a useful size.

Gypsophila **(Baby's breath)** The florets turn cream when pressed, but are still pretty. They make good centres for larger flowers.

Helianthemum **(Rock rose)** Delicate five-petalled flowers in a wide range of colours. All press well.

Helianthemum (Rock rose)

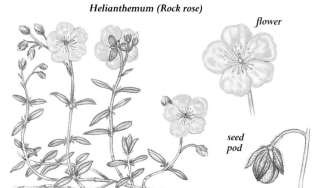

flower

seed pod

Heuchera **(Coral flower)** Press the delicate pink or red sprays on their long, curving stems.

Hydrangea Press as individual florets. All colours keep well.

Hypericum **(St John's wort)** The smaller varieties can be pressed whole, but the silky yellow stamens are also good pressed separately.

Limnanthes douglasii **(Poached egg flower)** The silvery-white and yellow flowers press extremely well.

Lobelia erinus The dark blue variety is one of the relatively few blue flowers which keeps it colour well.

Lonicera **(Honeysuckle)** Separate into individual florets. These have a tendancy to brown, but are a good shape.

Mimosa The little round flowers are a lovely yellow and an interesting shape. Press on short pieces of stem.

Mimulus **(Monkey flower)** Spotted, trumpet-shaped flowers in shades of yellow, burnt orange and red. All press well though the reds will darken considerably.

Myosotis **(Forget-me-not)** Can be pressed in sprays or separate florets. The latter are fiddly but very useful for small-scale designs.

Narcissus The smaller types such as 'Paper White' and 'Soleil d'Or' can be pressed whole. Larger daffodils can be cut in half and pressed in profile.

Nicotiana **(Tobacco plant)** Press flat, first removing the long green spur of the calyx. The green and white are good; the mauve turns a rich, deep purple.

Nigella damascena **(Love-in-a-mist)** Although the blue shades fade, the shape of flower and frondy foliage is so pretty that this is a must for the flower press.

Phlox Separate the heads and press as individual florets. Many colours available, but may fade.

Primula These days primulas come in a huge variety of shades all of which are worth experimenting with. Those with contrasting edges to their petals are particularly pretty.

Primula

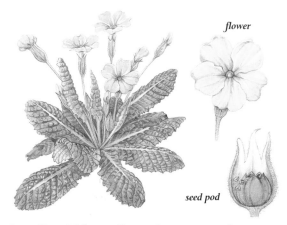

flower

seed pod

Rosa **(Rose)** The smaller single species are the easiest to press and keep their colour best. Snip off the hard seed-case behind the petals and press face down. Larger blooms need to be separated into individual petals, and may go brown.

Salvia horminum **(Clary)** The pink, purple and cream bracts keep their subtle colours well when pressed.

Solidago **(Golden rod)** A good yellow. Press in small sprays.

Statice **(Sea lavender)** A favourite dried flower, so as you would expect the colours are excellent. Press as separate florets.

Thymus serpyllum **(Thyme)** The tiny white and mauve flowers can be pressed in delicate sprays.

Tulipa **(Tulip)** The petals can be pressed separately or smaller flowers split in half and pressed in profile.

Viola x wittrockiana **(Pansy)** The smaller purple and yellow varieties, closest to their wild ancestors, are most useful and keep their colour best.

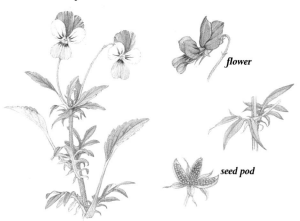

flower

seed pod

Viola x wittrockiana (Pansy)

Wild Flowers

Once upon a time none of us had any qualms about going out into the country and picking any wild flowers that took our fancy. Sadly, those days are gone. If we wish to preserve our wild flower heritage, we must be very careful about what we pick and where we pick it. Indeed, we are forbidden by law to pick a number of our rarest wild flowers (see appendix p.48).

Fortunately for the flower presser, many of the most suitable wild flowers for pressing are very common. Some, in fact, are the very weeds you are probably trying hard to banish from your garden. But even common wild flowers should only be picked in places where they are abundant, and a good proportion of flower heads should be left to set seed for another year. *If wild flowers are rare or scarce, do not pick them.*

An alternative is to grow your own wild flowers, and this is certainly the answer if you want to press declining species such as primroses or cowslips. Wild flower seed is now widely available, and you will have the satisfaction both of growing these lovely flowers and knowing that you are doing your bit for conservation.

The list below gives some wild flowers which you can almost always pick without too much concern.

Achillea millifolium **(Yarrow)** White or pinkish flat heads of flower. Both the flowers and the ferny leaves press well.

Anthriscus sylvestris **(Cow parsley)** Very common and extremely useful for its white lacy flowers. The seed heads are also good. Other similar members of the Umbelliferae (Carrot family) include fool's parsley (*Aethusa cynapium*) and the dreaded garden weed, ground elder (*Aegopodium podagraria*).

Bellis perennis **(Daisy)** The common lawn daisy is excellent for pressing and has the merit of flowering for most of the year.

Calystegia sepium **(Bindweed, Hedge)** A garden menace, but the big trumpet flowers are surprisingly effective when snipped in half and pressed flat.

Convolvulus arvensis **(Bindweed, Field)** Press short trails of these pink and white trumpet flowers with little oval leaves.

Epilobium angustifolium **(Rose-bay willowherb)** Deep purple-red flower spikes, common on waste ground. Press single flowers, buds and the tips of the flower spikes.

Geranium robertianum **(Herb Robert)** The delicate pinky-red flowers are very attractive as are the slender, pointed seedheads.

Ranunculus acris **(Buttercup)** One of the best yellow flowers to press: easy and very common.

Ranunculus ficaria **(Celandine)** A nice shape and a good yellow, which will gradually fade to silver.

leaves

Ranunculus ficaria (Celandine)

***Rosa canina* (Dog rose)** The single white or pink-flushed flowers are very effective pressed full face. Cut off the hard seedcase from behind the flower first.

flower

Rosa canina (Dog rose)

***Sambucus nigra* (Elder)** The creamy flower heads are too large to press individually, but are easy to divide.

***Senecio vulgaris* (Groundsel)** A common garden weed all year round. Press the tufted yellow flowers in profile.

***Trifolium repens* (Clover, white)** The heads dry beige but are still attractive on their curved stalks.

***Tussilago farfara* (Coltsfoot)** Another useful yellow flower of early spring. The flat, dandelion-like heads are easy to press.

***Vicia* (Vetch)** There are several common members of the vetch family. Most have blue or purple pea flowers and twining tendrils. Press flowers, leaves and twining stems.

Leaves

Most green deciduous leaves will turn brown or beige when pressed, so choose them for their shape rather than their colour.

Evergreens such as conifers and some herbs stay green, but only the finer varieties can be used. Many autumn leaves keep their beautiful yellow, bronze and red shades. Most grey and silver leaves will also keep their colour well.

***Acer* (Maple)** Use the finely divided leaves of the smaller Japanese maples, with their brilliant autumn colours.

Ameliancher Pick the leaves in autumn, when they are bright red.

***Anthriscus sylvestris* (Cow parsley)** The frondy leaves stay bright green if pressed when young.

Artemisia Press the foliage for its finely cut shape and excellent silver-grey colour.

Cineraria Very attractive lacy, silvery-white foliage.

Clematis The leaves and twining stems of *C. montana* turn black when pressed, and are very useful for both shape and colour.

***Cornus* (Dogwood)** The variegated leaves keep their colour well, especially when the green is just turning gold in autumn.

***Fagus sylvatica* (Beech)** Both the pale green young leaves and the bronze autumn foliage press well.

Geranium Many geraniums have interesting-shaped leaves which press well. Those of the wild cranesbill, Herb Robert, are especially delicate and have an attractive reddish tint in late summer and autumn.

Hellebore The palmate leaves dry to a good dark green.

Hellebore

flower

seed pod

Palmate leaves

***Jasminum officinalis* (Jasmine)** Delicate frondy leaves on curving stems.

***Juniperus* (Juniper)** The young foliage of the scale-leaved species stays dark green when pressed.

***Lavendula* (Lavender)** Press small sprigs. The narrow leaves are grey green and an attractive curved shape.

***Nepeta mussinnii* (Catmint)** Small, grey-green.

***Polygonum baldschuanicum* (Russian vine)** Good for its deep red autumn leaves.

Prunus (Flowering cherry) The leaves of most flowering cherries turn splendid shades of red and deep mahogany brown in autumn.

Quercus (Oak) Like beech, press the young leaves or the bronze-tinted autumn foliage.

Rhus cotinus (Smokebush) Rounded leaves of a lovely deep red with darker spots.

Rosemarinus (Rosemary) The leaves need some weight to press them, but the dark-green and silver spikes are most attractive.

Rubus idaeus (Raspberry) Useful for the greyish-silver undersides to the leaves.

Grasses

Although grasses may lack colour, their feathery curves can add another dimension to your pressed flower designs. Most grasses press well as they contain very little moisture. Pick them when the grass heads are young for best results. Some of the commonest wild grasses are the quaking grass (*Brizia media*), the common bent grass (*Agrostis tenuis*), and rough-stalked meadow grass (*Poa trivilis*). You might also try, for the leaves as much as the stems, the green and white striped ribbon grass (*Phalaris arundinacea 'Picta'*) found in many gardens.

Ferns

Most ferns press quite well and are a very attractive shape. Larger fronds can be divided before pressing. Three of the commonest ferns are bracken (*Pteridium aquilinum*), found on heaths and in woodland; the male fern (*Dryopterisc felix-mas*), found in heaths and woodlands; and maidenhair spleenwort (*Asplenium trichomanes*) which grows in walls and rock crevices.

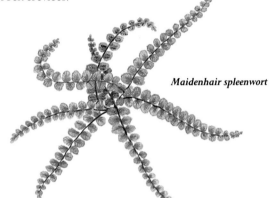

Maidenhair spleenwort

Seaweeds

Pressing seaweeds was a favourite pastime of Victorian ladies, and their seaweed pictures can still sometimes be found in antique shops. There is no reason why you should not use seaweeds too, provided you only take them where they are plentiful. Choose only the smaller and more delicate sorts, wash them well to remove the sand and saltwater, drain and pat dry between several sheets of kitchen paper. Then lay out the fronds on blotting paper in an attractive shape and press in the normal way. Take great care when removing the seaweeds from the blotting paper as they can be very brittle when dried.

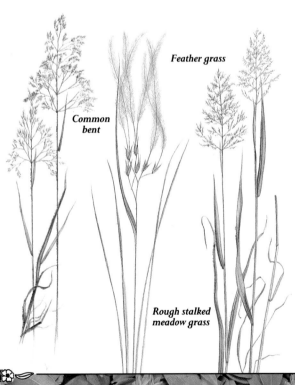

Feather grass

Common bent

Rough stalked meadow grass

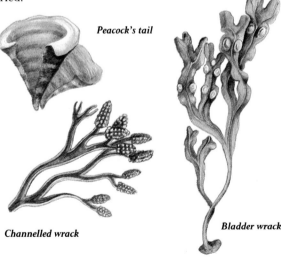

Peacock's tail

Channelled wrack

Bladder wrack

PRESSED FLOWER DESIGN

SHAPES AND COLOURS

*T*he main inspiration in creating a pressed flower design will be the beautiful colours and shapes of the flowers and leaves themselves. However, when you first come to make up a design and are faced with a collection of pressed flowers and a blank sheet of paper it is useful to have some guidelines to follow. There are two important things you will want to consider: the first is the shape of your pressed flower design, the second is its colour.

The texture of plant material can also play an important part in the making up of designs. Feathery leaves, coarse moss, rough bark, spiky grass, will all form interesting contrasts to the flowers themselves.

Start with something simple such as a greetings card or bookmark; there are plenty of ideas for both on pages 30 to 32. As you gain confidence in the techniques involved you will be ready to tackle bigger projects such as pressed flower pictures.

SHAPE

The underlying shape of a design is very important. However attractive your pressed flowers may be, if they are arranged haphazardly it is more than likely that they will just look a mess.

Geometric Shapes

One of the simplest ideas is to base a design on simple, regular geometric shapes: for example a circle, a triangle, an oval, a star or a diamond. You will probably not, in the end, follow it exactly, but a strong shape will give a good base to build round.

Letters

Using letters as the base of a design is another simple idea and particularly appropriate for greetings cards, gift boxes and small pictures.

Natural Shapes

An alternative to basing your designs on geometric shapes is to make up simple representational designs. One of the simplest and prettiest ideas is to arrange flowers to form a posy or a bouquet, perhaps tied with a 'ribbon' of grass or a real ribbon. Or you could create a vase of flowers – the vase itself can be cut from a leaf or made from two or three large petals. As you become more experienced, try copying a favourite flower painting. Don't worry if the flowers you have are not the same; just try to give an idea of the shapes and colours in the painting.

An idea requiring a good selection of leaves, stems and grasses, is to create miniature landscapes. Use frondy leaves and ferns for trees and ribbons of grass to outline hills. Other leaf shapes may suggest birds or animals, and the delicately veined petals of a flower such as a geranium (crane's bill) would make beautiful butterflies.

This collection of designs show the different effects achieved using even the simplest of shapes.

COLOUR

Pressed flowers do not have the same strength of colour as fresh flowers; their colours are usually subtler and more muted. There should not be a problem of colours clashing; but some thought does need to be given to the use of colour in a design to make it really effective.

The first thing to decide is whether you are going to aim for colour harmony or colour contrast. Contrasting colours are those from opposite ends of the colour spectrum. They throw each other into sharp relief, whilst harmonising colours blend together.

Colours are divided into primary and secondary colours. The primary colours are red, yellow and blue; the secondary colours result from mixing the primary colours. So red and yellow give orange, yellow and blue give green, and red and blue give violet. As a rule, two primary colours and the colour produced by mixing them will all blend happily together. So red, orange and yellow flowers will be happy together, as will red, violet and blue flowers, or blue and yellow flowers with green leaves.

In fact green, as in nature, will tone with all your arrangements provided it is not too vivid a shade (which is very unlikely with pressed material). White, silver and cream will also mix well with any colours, giving a softening and cooling effect.

Pastel shades are the easiest to blend together. Strong colours need to be treated with more caution, but can be tremendously effective. The same applies to the colour of your backing material. For example, a soft, pastel-coloured design of pinks, blues and mauves would look attractive on a pale green or cream ground, whereas a rich-toned arrangement of gold and red autumn leaves might look stunning on black, or white flowers and silver leaves on deep red.

Remember, though, that rules are made to be broken and it is what pleases your eye that counts.

MAKING UP A DESIGN

Whether you are making up a simple greeting card or an elaborate flower picture, you will follow this basic procedure. Collect together everything on this checklist before you begin work.

Equipment checklist	
Pressed flowers and plants *(for protection, keep them in their storage books or files until you are just about to use them)*	Glue
	Tools *(tweezers, cocktail sticks, paintbrush, cotton buds etc.)*
	Scissors and craft knife
Backing material: *card, paper or fabric*	Wooden or plastic board
Drawing paper and pencil	Old newspapers or sheet of oilcloth

1 Setting up

Make sure you have enough space to work in with room for everything you are going to need from the time you begin work to the moment the flowers are firmly stuck down on their backing.

A complicated design may take some time, so try to work where the design can be left undisturbed if you have to break off.

Collect together everything you are going to need to make up a design before you start work.

2 Choosing the flowers

There are two ways to begin a design – choose the flowers first and build a design around them or choose a design and then select the appropriate flowers. If you have a good collection of flowers and leaves already pressed, it's probably best to decide on the design and then pick out the most suitable flowers to use. If your stock is limited, try taking selection of flowers and foliage and placing them on a plain piece of paper to see what ideas suggest themselves: also see the design suggestions on pp22-3.

This 'free form' method is the way in which many experienced people create their pressed flower pictures and you may find it the easiest and most satisfactory way.

The variety of flowers and foliage in your collection will be a major source of inspiration in the planning of any design.

3 Sketching the design

If you are not copying or interpreting an existing design, it's a good idea to sketch out your idea on a piece of paper – roughly, but to scale. If the design is at all complicated it is helpful to pencil faint key points of the design on to the backing material, in the form of dots or small crosses. This will ensure that the design is centred properly on its background – the marks themselves will, of course, be hidden by the flowers.

A rough outline of the proposed design will make it much easier to put together and help to achieve a balanced looking design.

4 The background material

The background material for a pressed flower design can be plain or coloured paper or card, or fabric. Fabric backings are especially pretty for substantial items such as pressed flower pictures and paperweights. The fabrics used should be plain in colour and not too thick or heavily textured. Natural fibres such as silk, good quality cotton and fine cotton velvet are more satisfactory than man-made fibres, which are often too slippery and shiny.

The selected background material needs to be cut to size and, if necessary, reinforced. Card can be used just as it is, but both paper and fabric will need some additional stiffening. Paper can be glued on to thin card. Fabric should be backed by card or by a foam pad, depending on the frame or setting you propose to use (*see* Frames and mounts pp42-43).

Choose the background to each design with care. The right background will enhance a design enormously.

Place the glue as near as possible to the centre of the item you are sticking down, so that no excess squeezes out round the edge. If this does happen, a cotton bud can be used to dab the glue away.

Use the minimum amount of glue on each item to prevent glue from seeping from underneath flowers.

5 *Moving flowers into position*

To begin to assemble the design place flowers in position using blunt-nose tweezers. The point of a cocktail stick or the tip of a paintbrush may be helpful in moving the flowers around. Try not to handle the flowers too much as they are quite fragile. Move everything into the right position but do not glue anything down at this stage.

Build up your design gradually and ensure that everything is in the right position before gluing anything down.

6 *Gluing the design in place*

Once your design is complete and you are happy with it, you are ready to glue the flowers in position. It is easiest to start gluing from the outside of the design and work inwards. Lift each flower or piece of foliage individually, apply the glue and place it carefully back in position before moving on to the next flower.

Use only the smallest amount of glue (a latex adhesive, such as Copydex, is the most suitable). Put a small amount of glue into a shallow container, this will make it easier and less messy to use. Apply it with the tip of a cocktail stick to the reverse of the flower or leaf at its thickest point. A couple of tiny blobs will hold most flowers in place; larger leaves may require a little more, glue for larger areas can be applied with a cotton bud. Stems and grasses will need several tiny spots of glue down their entire length.

7 Covering the design

As a rule, all pressed flower designs need to be covered to protect them from damage, dust and damp. The coverings most commonly used are self-adhesive film, acetate film, glass and varnish. The use of glass for flower pictures is covered in the section on framing on pages 42-43. Self-adhesive film and acetate are suitable for simpler items such as cards, gift tags, bookmarks and so on.

Acetate film simply needs to be cut to size and glued over the design using a thin line of glue round the edge. Alternatively, it can be glued on to the reverse of a mount to form a 'window', which is then stuck over the design.

Self-adhesive film is trickier to use. Cut a piece to size and lay it over the design then, working from one corner, carefully peel away the backing and press the film down, rubbing all the time with a soft cloth to make sure there are no air bubbles. Be especially careful to rub it down well when placing it over thicker leaves and stems. The matt variety of film shows up imperfections less than the shiny sort. When using the film, try not to pick up bits of grit and loose material which will spoil the end result.

Heat-sensitive film This is a self-adhesive film which will not stick unless heated with a cool iron. With practice, very good results can be achieved with it.

Varnish can be used to protect designs on more solid items such as table mats or decorative boxes. Use a clear polyurethane varnish, cover the surface of the item to be decorated with a thin coat and then arrange your flowers on it (no glue is needed of course). Leave to dry and then carefully paint on as many coats of varnish as are necessary to cover the design, letting each coat dry before applying the next.

Pressed flower designs are quite delicate and need to be protected. Varnish and the various types of film are ideal for covering quite small areas.

PRESSED FLOWERS FOR DECORATION

There are so many decorative ways in which pressed flowers can be used, and this section is full of ideas. It begins with relatively simple items such as greeting cards, gift tags and bookmarks, which show how easy it is to achieve very pretty effects with a limited range of flowers and foliage.

A range of attractive and useful gift and household items comes next. They include candles, paperweights, door finger plates, decorated books and a selection of gift boxes. Nowadays many craft shops, as well as mail order suppliers, sell giftware ranges which are specially designed to display craftwork and these are ideal for pressed flower designs.

The section on pressed flower pictures of different styles gives a glimpse of the 'art' of pressed flowers. It is becoming increasingly popular for a bride to have the flowers from her bridal bouquet pressed as a wedding day memento. There are delightful examples here of pictures made from wedding day flowers, plus instructions on how to tackle this specialised task.

These pages show just some of the many ways in which pressed flowers can be used for decoration. But they can also be used to decorate jewellery, mirrors, vases, lampshades, even small pieces of furniture – the possibilities are virtually endless. All you need is a little bit of imagination, and I hope that the ideas here will encourage you to enjoy making your own experiments and discoveries.

GREETING CARDS

Pressed flower greeting cards are always welcome. Far too
pretty to throw away, they can be kept and framed as
treasured reminders of a special day. An especially
attractive idea is to personalise your card with the
recipient's initial, picked out in the smallest, most delicate
flowers you can find.

Card bases specifically for this purpose can be bought
from craft shops but they are quite straightforward to
make.

Simple cards

1 Trim the paper to the overall size required and fold it
  in half.
2 A simple ink border or perhaps even a lace edging will
  help to give the design more form.
3 Cover the design with self-adhesive film.

Window cards

1 Decide on the dimensions for the front panel of the
  card and cut the paper or card to three times this
  width. Fold the card in three.
2 Cut out whatever shaped window you have decided on
  from the centre third of the card. Leave an adequate
  frame around the window. The window will need to be
  regular so use rulers, set squares, compasses or
  whatever is appropriate to give the best result. Use a
  sharp craft knife to cut
  out the window.
3 Glue an acetate covering
  to the underneath of
  the window.
4 Position your design on
  the piece of card
  beneath the window.
5 Glue the window panel
  to the design panel.

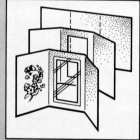

Insert cards

An insert can be placed inside a coloured card base to give
a contrasting colour in the window of the card.
1 Cut a piece of coloured card as if making a simple card.
2 Cut a contrasting piece of paper or thin card to a
  fractionally smaller size so that it can be inserted into
  the first card and its edges cannot be seen.
3 Cut the window shape from the outer card and fix an
  acetate covering.
4 Place the design in the right position on the insert card
  and glue the two panels together.

GIFT TAGS

A pretty gift tag decorated with pressed flowers adds a thoughtful finishing touch to any present. This is also a good way to use up any small oddments of flowers which don't fit into a larger design.

Gift tags are very easy to make and can be made using any of the principles used to make greetings cards. Even simpler gift tags can be made by just cutting pieces of card to different shapes: simple geometric shapes, letters, numbers or, if it is a Christmas gift, perhaps a holly leaf or Christmas tree.

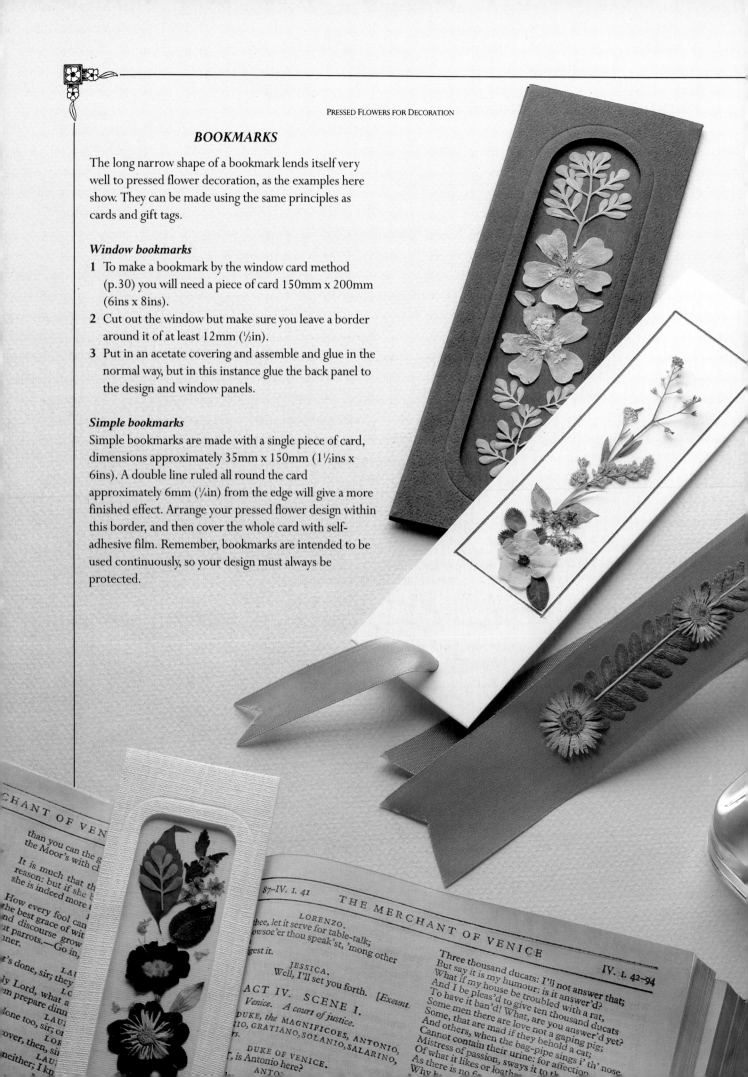

BOOKMARKS

The long narrow shape of a bookmark lends itself very
well to pressed flower decoration, as the examples here
show. They can be made using the same principles as
cards and gift tags.

Window bookmarks

1 To make a bookmark by the window card method
   (p.30) you will need a piece of card 150mm x 200mm
   (6ins x 8ins).
2 Cut out the window but make sure you leave a border
   around it of at least 12mm (½in).
3 Put in an acetate covering and assemble and glue in the
   normal way, but in this instance glue the back panel to
   the design and window panels.

Simple bookmarks

Simple bookmarks are made with a single piece of card,
dimensions approximately 35mm x 150mm (1½ins x
6ins). A double line ruled all round the card
approximately 6mm (¼in) from the edge will give a more
finished effect. Arrange your pressed flower design within
this border, and then cover the whole card with self-
adhesive film. Remember, bookmarks are intended to be
used continuously, so your design must always be
protected.

PAPERWEIGHTS

Pressed flower paperweights make charming gifts. Keep the designs simple and for an especially pretty effect use a piece of fabric (silk, satin or very fine velvet are all ideal) as the design base.

Undecorated glass paperweights can be bought in most craft shops. They come in a range of shapes and sizes, several of which are illustrated here. Most are sold complete with design base and backing, although you may have to supply these yourself.

To make up a paperweight, if backing and insert card is not supplied:

1 Cut a piece of card to fit the recess of the paperweight. If you are using a fabric as a background, cut it to the same size as the card and glue them together.

2 Arrange the design on to the base as usual and glue it in place.

3 Cut a piece of self-adhesive green baize large enough to cover the whole base of the paperweight (this is available from craft shops – if you cannot obtain it, self-adhesive film can be used instead).

4 Fit the design on its backing gently into the paperweight recess. Turn the paperweight over so that the glass is downwards and stick the baize or film over the back, so that the design is held securely in place.

DOOR FINGER PLATES

Door finger plates, like bookmarks, are a good shape for pressed flower designs. The clear perspex plates can be bought from both craft shops and hardware stores.

1 Cut a piece of card to fit the recess in the plate. If the recess is deep, back the card with a piece of foam. If there is no recess, cut it approximately 6mm (¼in) smaller than the plate all round.

2 Arrange the flowers and foliage on the card and glue them into position.

3 Position the card in the recess of the plate or on the back of the plate, making sure there is an even border all round. Back with self-adhesive film.

ADDRESS BOOKS AND DIARIES

Pressed flower decoration makes an ordinary address book, diary or notebook that little bit special. The design must be protected if the book is to be used regularly, and the easiest way to do this is to use self-adhesive film (the matt variety is the most satisfactory).

1 Arrange the pressed flower design on the cover of the book and then glue it into position as normal.

2 If the design only covers a small area, cut a piece of film a little larger than the design and stick it down over the design, taking care to press out any air bubbles.

3 If the design covers a large area, cut a piece of film the size of the book's front cover plus a 12mm (½in) overlap on three sides. Stick the film down over the whole cover, tucking in the overlap on the top, bottom and right-hand sides. This is most suitable for small books, as large areas of self-adhesive film are quite difficult to handle.

CANDLES

Large plain candles look most effective decorated with pressed flowers. Keep your design simple and arrange it round the base, so that as the candle burns it does not destroy the flowers too quickly. If you can find the sort of thick candles which only burn down in the middle, so much the better. Choose flowers and leaves that are not too bulky.

Design held in place by glue

This is the simplest method but you must not let the candle burn down to the design as both the glue and the flowers are inflammable. It is best to arrange the design around the base of the candle.

1 Glue the flowers using a latex glue.

2 The design can then be covered with self-adhesive film. This will make the candle look smoother but it is essential that the film does not catch fire as it will give off unpleasant fumes and burn to a sticky mess.

Design held in place by wax

This is a more complicated method but it does mean that the candle can burn more safely.

1 Melt some candlewax (enough to coat the candle several times) in a deep saucepan. Dip the candle into the melted wax — hold it by the wick. Allow it to cool and then dip again.

2 Allow the candle to cool a little and press the flowers in place. Brush the design area with melted wax. Cool.

3 Dip the candle once more into the wax. When the candle is completely cool polish it with a soft tissue.

GIFT BOXES

Pretty pots and boxes decorated with pressed flowers always make welcome presents. Undecorated porcelain, glass or wooden containers are available from many gift and craft shops as well as mail order suppliers. Also obtainable are giftware ranges with lids specially designed to display craftwork, these are ideal for pressed flower arrangements.

Boxes with glass lids

These kits, some of which are illustrated here, contain everything you need to complete your designs. Just arrange the flowers on the backing sheet provided, glue them into position and then assemble the box according to the manufacturer's instructions. Alternatively, the backing could be replaced with a piece of coloured card or fabric cut to the same size.

Plain boxes

Boxes without these special lids can also be decorated with pressed flowers. Here varnish is used to give the pressed flower design lasting protection. Simply glue the flowers into position on the box, then carefully paint two or three coats of clear household varnish over them. Allow each coat of varnish to dry before applying another. The hexagonal glass pot pourri holder shown here has been decorated in this way and this technique can also be used on porcelain, wood and sturdy card boxes.

A WEDDING BOUQUET

A pressed flower picture made from the flowers in a wedding bouquet makes a lovely memento of a special day, and more and more brides are choosing to have their wedding flowers preserved in this way. This is quite a complicated task, as wedding flowers are not always ideal for pressing, and some people may prefer to have it done professionally to be sure of a good result. However, once you are reasonably confident of your pressing techniques there is no reason why you should not tackle the job yourself, following the same steps as you would when creating any flower picture.

If you are ordering a wedding bouquet and intend to press it, do bear in mind that some flowers are more suitable than others.

The following usually press well:

Carnations
Roses } *deeper shades are better than white and cream*
Freesia
Alstromeria
Gypsophila
Asparagus fern

The following are less reliable:
Orchids
Stephanotis
Chrysanthemums
Lilies

The following points are important when pressing a wedding bouquet:

1 When you order the bouquet, ask the florist not to wire the flower heads. If they are wired, you will end up with ugly rusty holes in the petals.

2 Make sure the florist does not spray the bouquet before delivery; once damp the flowers will never dry properly and will not press well.

3 If you intend to follow the design of the bouquet have a close-up photograph of it taken for later reference.

4 If you cannot dismantle the bouquet and put the flowers in the press immediately after the wedding, put it in the fridge as soon as possible. It should keep fresh for a maximum of 3-4 days.

5 Press all suitable flowers from the bouquet and don't forget to press plenty of leaves and stems. Although you are unlikely to use every flower for the bride's picture, extra flowers can be made up into smaller pictures for the bride's mother, mother-in-law and the bridesmaids.

6 Wedding pictures are traditionally backed with the same fabric as the bride's or bridesmaids' dresses. If this is not possible, white or pastel-coloured silks and satins are the most suitable backing.

PRESSED FLOWER PICTURES

The creation of pressed flower pictures is an art in its own right and, with experience, this is perhaps the most satisfying way of all to use the wonderful colours and shapes of pressed flowers and foliage. Picture styles are as varied as the people who make them, but the varied selection of pictures on these pages should give you both inspiration and a good idea of what can be achieved. For some practical help, turn to the design guidelines on pages 21-25 and the framing section on pages 42-43.

Remember that pressed flower pictures should never be hung where they will be exposed to a lot of sunlight as they will fade.

Above this simple, almost crude, bowl of
flowers has a lively, modern feeling.
Right different coloured leaves are used to great effect
to create this magnificent-looking bird.

These miniature pictures are on backgrounds of silky fabrics. They make charming inexpensive presents.

FRAMES AND MOUNTS

A well-chosen frame and mount can add much to the beauty of a pressed flower picture. As you will see in the illustrations on pages 40-41, flower pictures can be framed in many different ways, both with and without mounts. There is a huge range of frames to choose from: rectangular, oval (a particularly pretty shape for a flower picture), round, square, painted, gilded, plain wood, metal, simple or elaborate, old or new. Your own taste, and the amount of money you have to spend, will dictate what you use. Personally, I think that simple frames in natural materials – plain wood, painted or softly gilded – suit the charm of pressed flowers better than shiny metal or lots of elaborate beading.

The following points need to be borne in mind when selecting frames and mounts:

Mounts

* Mounts should be made of thin card or paper to allow the flowers to be up against the glass of the frame. Lines drawn around the mount will give a feeling of depth.
* Thick mounting card can be used if the design has a fabric background which can be backed with foam. This will allow the design to be pushed some way through the mount.

Frames

* The frame must be airtight and the glass must fit closely over the flowers leaving no gap between them.
* The rebate, the groove in the frame which holds glass, mount and picture, must be deep enough to hold all the material.
* Before beginning a design either buy a frame or have some idea of an obtainable frame size in mind. Otherwise you may find you have a beautiful design and no frame to put it in.
* If possible fit the frame with non-reflective glass.

Frames can be obtained from a variety of sources but bear in mind the above points when selecting a frame.
Professional frames are almost certain to be highly satisfactory but can be quite expensive. It may be worth using a professional framer for very special pictures such as bridal bouquets.
Do-it-yourself frames come in all shapes and sizes and are widely available. They are usually very straightforward to put together. Small frames are available designed specifically to display pressed flowers and embroidery.

Old frames can be found in antique and junk shops and at antique fairs and the like. The frames may need a little tidying up but are often more keeping with the old-world charm of pressed flower pictures.

Frames, whatever their source, are normally put together in the same way:

How to assemble a picture frame

1 Clean the glass thoroughly and fit it into the frame.

2 Place the glass and frame face-down. Fit the mount, if used, into the frame behind the glass.

3 Check that the flower picture is properly glued down and that there is no loose material or dust on its surface.

4 Lay the picture, face down, on to the glass. If you are using a card mount and fabric backing, push the picture gently from behind so that it is pressed up firmly against the glass.

5 Place the hardboard backing behind the picture and check that it holds it firmly against the glass. If it does not, cut some extra backing such as a double sheet of blotting paper or a piece of thin foam and place it between picture and board.

6 Fix the hardboard into position. Clips are usually provided for this with ready-made frames. Alternatively you can use panel pins, gently knocked in with a hammer.

7 Tape all round the back of the picture where the hardboard meets the frame, covering the join and making a good seal.

8 Using a gimlet make holes on either side of the frame. Screw in the hooks and attach the picture wire or cord to the back of the frame.

This striking picture has a bright blue silk background with a foam padding to give a feeling of depth. The oval frame is made of a contrasting rich dark wood.

PRESSED FLOWERS FOR CHILDREN

F lower pressing has always been a popular hobby for children, although once the flowers have been pressed the child is often left wondering what to do next. These pages should answer that question. They show simple, inexpensive and enjoyable ideas for using pressed flowers and foliage which are suitable for younger children to undertake with a minimum of supervision (all the items shown here were made by two children aged six and eight, with a little guidance from their mother). Older children may like to start pressed flower work with some of these suggestions, but they will find many of the ideas in the section on Pressed Flowers for Decoration well within their scope.

Calendar

It is best if the flowers to be used by younger children are large and reasonably robust, as they may not be dexterous enough to handle delicate blooms. Leaves and grasses are especially suitable as are everlasting flowers of various kinds. As the designs will not normally be covered it doesn't matter if the material used is bulkier than usual.

Clear varnish, is the best covering for children to use, if they are old enough to handle a paintbrush with reasonable ease. Varnish suitable for use by children is available from craft shops. When children are using varnish or sticking flowers down with glue, it's a good idea to give them just a small quantity in a container such as a saucer or ramekin dish. This will limit the amount of sticky mess caused if there's an accident. Any working surface should be covered with plenty of old newspapers for the same reason!

BIG AND BOLD DESIGNS

Most children have a surprisingly good sense of design,
but some initial pointers on working techniques will be
helpful.

1 First, select the design backing and then suggest that
   the child picks out a selection of flowers and foliage to
   use *before* starting to arrange them.

2 Explain that it's a good idea to lay these out on the
   backing and play around with some ideas before the
   design is stuck down. To keep the backing clean, it may
   be helpful to do this on a sheet of scrap paper and then
   transfer the flowers to the backing when the design is
   complete.

3 Show the child how to stick the design in position
   using the minimum of glue, applied in small spots with
   a cocktail stick or the tip of a paintbrush.

4 Show how to lift up one flower at a time and glue it
   down without disturbing the rest of the design.

If you bear these points in mind you should have lots of
fun and, I hope, some very successful results.

DECORATED PEBBLES

These decorated pebbles are simple and fun to make; they
can be used as doorstops, paperweights, or simply as
decoration.

   The technique is very straightforward:

1 Clean and dry the stones.

2 Decide on your design and then apply a coat of varnish
   to the design area. Press the flowers into position on
   top of the varnish.

3 When everything is in position apply more coats of
   varnish, waiting for each layer to dry before applying
   the next. The design should be completely covered
   with everything held in place.

$\mathcal{I}$ NDEX

PROTECTED WILD FLOWERS

The following wild flowers are protected by law in England, Scotland and Wales. Listing courtesy of the Nature Conservancy Council. (A separate list is available for Northern Ireland).

Adder's-tongue Spearwort
Alpine Blue Sow-thistle
Alpine Catchfly
Alpine Fleabane
Alpine Gentian
Alpine Rock-cress
Alpine Woodsia
Arctic/English Sandwort
Bedstraw Broomrape
Blue Heath
Branched Horsetail
Bristol Rock-cress
Brown Galingale
Cambridge Milk-parsley
Cheddar Pink
Childing Pink
Creeping Marshwort
Cut-leaved Germander
Diapensia
Dickie's Bladder-fern
Downy Woundwort
Drooping Saxifrage
Early Spider Orchid
Early Star-of-Bethlehem
Fen Orchid
Fen Ragwort
Fen Violet
Field Cow-wheat
Field Eryngo
Field Wormwood
Fingered Speedwell
Fox-tail Stonewort
Fringed Gentian
Ghost Orchid
Grass-poly
Greater Yellow-rattle
Green Hound's-tongue
Holly-leaved Naiad
Jersey Cudweed
Killarney Fern
Lady's Slipper
Late Spider Orchid
Least Adder's-tongue
Least Lettuce
Limestone Woundwort
Lizard Orchid

Lundy Cabbage
Martin's Ramping Fumitory
Military Orchid
Monkey Orchid
Oblong Woodsia
Oxtongue Broomrape
Pennyroyal
Perennial Knawel
Pigmyweed
Plymouth Pear
Purple Colt's-foot
Purple Spurge
Red Helleborine
Red-tipped Cudweed
Ribbon-leaved Water-plantain
Rock Cinquefoil
Rock Sea-lavender
Rough Marsh-mallow
Round-headed Leek
Sand Crocus
Sea Knotgrass
Sickle-leaved Hare's-ear
Slender Cottongrass
Small Alison
Small Fleabane
Small Hare's-ear
Small Restharrow
Snowdon Lily
Spiked Speedwell
Spring Gentian
Starfruit
Starved Wood Sedge
Stinking Goosefoot
Stinking Hawk's-beard
Strapwort
Thistle Broomrape
Tufted Saxifrage
Triangular Club-rush
Teesdale Sandwort
Viper's Grass
Water Germander
Whorled Solomon's-seal
Wild Cotoneaster
Wild Gladiolus
Wood Calamint
Young's Helleborine

MAIL ORDER SUPPLIERS

Impress
Slough Farm, Westhall, Halesworth, Suffolk 1P19 8RN, England
Ready-to-use pressed flowers; blank cards, bookmarks, gift tags, etc.; self-adhesive film, felt and other materials for pressed flower work.

Framecraft Miniatures Ltd
148-150 High Street, Aston, Birmingham B6 4US, England
Frames, gift boxes, paperweights and a wide range of other items for displaying handicrafts.

ACKNOWLEDGEMENTS

This book would not have been possible without the help and advice of a number of people. I should like to thank: Denise Hodge and Elsie James for producing many of the designs illustrated in these pages, also Iris Homes; Nicholas and Maria Adey and their mother, Kate, for the children's designs; Fiona Mavor for books, plants and flowers; Kate Miles for her help with microwaving. Finally, thanks to Sylvia Benstead of Not Fade Away, 29 Cyprus Road, Cambridge for the wedding bouquet picture, the picture on page 44 and gift boxes.

The publishers would like to thank Langford and Hill Ltd, Warwick St, London W1 for supplying graphic materials; Frames, 73 Forest Road, Loughton, Essex for supplying frames and mounts; Angela Flanders for supplying dried flowers and pot pourri & Chas Wilder of Paramount for his photographic assistance.